DIGITAL CAREER BUILDING™

CAREER BUILDING THROUGH

USING DIGITAL PUBLISHING TOOLS

REBECCA T. KLEIN

ROSEN PUBLISHING®

New York

Published in 2014 by The Rosen Publishing Group, Inc.
29 East 21st Street, New York, NY 10010

Library of Congress Cataloging-in-Publication Data

Klein, Rebecca T.
Career building through using digital publishing tools/by Rebecca T. Klein—1st ed.
    p. cm.—(Digital career building)
Includes index and bibliography.
ISBN 978-1-4777-1724-0 (library binding)—
ISBN 978-1-4777-1741-7 (pbk.)—ISBN 978-1-4777-1742-4 (6-pack)
1. Electronic publishing—Vocational guidance—Juvenile literature.
2. Authorship—Vocational guidance—Juvenile literature. 3. Social media—Juvenile literature. I.Klein, Rebecca T. II. Title.
Z286.E43 K52 2014
070.573—d23

Manufactured in the United States of America

CPSIA Compliance Information: Batch #W14YA: For further information, contact Rosen Publishing, New York, New York, at 1-800-237-9932.

CONTENTS

CHAPTER ONE

WHAT IS DIGITAL PUBLISHING?

For people who have grown up in the digital age, it is difficult to imagine a world without digital, or electronic, publishing. In fact, this phenomenon is so widespread that it may be something you don't even think about. Its definition, however, is fairly self-explanatory; the term "digital publishing" refers to books, articles, and other content being made available to the public through electronic, rather than print, sources. It includes e-books, blogs, online news sources, and electronic academic journals.

Before digital publishing, if a person wanted to carry twenty books around, he or she needed a big bag and a very strong back. Now a Kindle, a Nook, or an iPad can carry those same twenty books. Before digital pub-

E-readers make it easy and convenient to carry many books around at once and to read them anywhere. This is one reason why these devices are so popular.

lishing, in order to make art, poetry, and other kinds of media available to the public, a beginning artist or writer had to paste things together, type things up, and make physical copies to distribute. Now many artists and writers share their work through blogs or personal Web sites. Before digital publishing, writing an academic research paper meant spending hours in the library stacks, searching dusty books and physical copies of journals for articles that pertained to your topic. Now students conduct the bulk of their research online, browsing electronic journals and other sources. Digital publishing has completely transformed the way that information is gathered and shared.

Not only has digital publishing changed the way that art and information are distributed, it also has created a new field of industry and occupation. In order for things to be published electronically, there must be programs, called digital publishing tools, to make this possible. There are jobs for people who design these tools, as well as jobs for people who are experts at using them. Career opportunities that involve digital publishing include graphic design and computer programming. Also, any aspiring writer or artist needs to know how to use digital publishing to distribute his or her work to the widest audience possible. The following sections will explore the careers of people who have used digital publishing to advance their success and will discuss ways in which you can use digital publishing tools to build your own career. But first, here is a brief look at how digital publishing developed and how it currently functions.

History of Digital Publishing

The first great shift in the way that information was distributed occurred with the invention of the printing press by Johannes Gutenberg in the mid-fifteenth century. The printing press made it possible to make and sell books on a large scale, and to distribute information to the masses, rather than keeping it in the hands of the religious and political elite. It can be argued that digital publishing has created a similar shift. In addition to making the product (the books, the magazines, and the information itself) even more widely available, digital publishing has also shifted the actual means of production into the hands of the masses. It is easier than ever

The invention of the printing press in the mid-fifteenth century allowed many copies of books to be printed at once, making information available on a larger scale than it had ever been before.

before to share one's ideas, opinions, knowledge, and art with the world.

The history of digital publishing began in 1971, when Michael Hart invented electronic books (e-books) and started a large collection of e-books that are free to the public. Presumably seeing the connection between his own efforts and Gutenberg's invention of the printing press, Hart named this library Project Gutenberg. Starting out small, this collection began to grow quickly when the World Wide Web went public in the 1990s. Today, Project Gutenberg holds tens of thousands of books in its own collection, all of which are in the public domain.

QUICK TIP When the copyright on a book or any other type of intellectual property, such as a film or a piece of music, expires and is not renewed, it goes into the public domain. This means that it can be reproduced without having to obtain permission from an author or publisher. Many classic works of literature are in the public domain.

This paved the way for many other digital libraries, and Michael Hart's invention of the e-book format led many publishers to begin making some of their books available electronically. With the dawn of e-readers such as Amazon's Kindle and Barnes & Noble's Nook, e-books became even more popular. Today, there are some publishers and authors who bypass print altogether and release books in digital format exclusively.

CHECK IT OUT Project Gutenberg is located at www.gutenberg .org. You can find thousands of books there, fiction and nonfiction, which you can browse and read completely free of charge!

Other types of publications took advantage of the rise of digital publishing, too. In the 1990s, when the World Wide Web was new, many people had computers at home but did not have them connected to the Internet. Therefore, many magazines and reference sources published works on CD-ROM so that users could access digital files without needing the Internet. But when it became common for most households to have an Internet connection, the CD-ROM format became somewhat obsolete. Although there are still some publi-

These days most digitally published materials are published online, but before it was common for people to have Internet connections in their homes, CD-ROMs gave digital access to things like journals and encyclopedias.

cations available on CD-ROM, these days most people access digital files online, or download them directly onto a computer or mobile device. Also, many magazines and news sources publish content directly through blogs and other Web sites, so readers do not have to download files at all. With the wide use of e-readers and other handheld devices (such as cell phones and tablets) that connect to the Internet, digital publications are more convenient than ever.

What Will Become of Print Media?

There is no doubt that digital publishing has made many things more convenient, and no doubt that information is more readily available and easier to gather through digital sources. But is there still a place for print media, such as physical books, newspapers, and magazines? These days, it is rare to see someone carrying or using a CD player, and most stores have a minimal selection of CDs available for purchase. Since it is so much more convenient to carry all of your music on one device, the CD format has become

Newsweek magazine published its last print issue in December 2012 and switched to an entirely digital format. Many other news sources have done the same, and the future of print media is uncertain.

all but obsolete. Will this happen to books, newspapers, and magazines, too? Already, more space in bookstores is being devoted to electronic reading devices and related merchandise, and less space is dedicated to print books. But the advancement of digital publishing does not necessarily indicate the death of print. As Graydon Carter, editor at *Vanity Fair* magazine, colorfully asserts, "Not every media revolution ends with one combatant lifeless on the ground, blood trickling from his mouth. Television didn't kill radio. It just changed it." Obviously, digital media is changing the role of print. But there are still many people who value the experience of holding a physical copy of a book and underlining or highlighting their favorite passages. Although an increasing number of people prefer to read their news online, there are still those who like to sit at the kitchen table with a newspaper or magazine, rather than a laptop. Although most people turn to digital sources for daily news and lots of casual reading, many still prefer to do their serious reading in print format. It will be interesting to see if this remains true in a couple of generations.

Digital Publishing's Current Uses

One of the places where digital publishing has made a huge impact is in the academic world. E-books, online databases, and electronic journals have completely changed the way that students conduct research. Before digital publishing, students gathered information from physical books, either photocopying pages or writing quotations in notebooks and on index cards. But when you write an assignment for school, chances are that you go straight to the Internet first and consult print sources as a second option, if you consult them at all.

Digital publishing is also a social phenomenon. Many people these days publish their own writings and artwork regularly through blogs or other Web sites. You may do this yourself, or you may know other people your age who do it. Blogging can be a great way to stay connected with people you know and to share your work and thoughts with friends and family. If you choose to go public, it is a convenient way to expose your work to a wider audience.

Digital publishing, especially the publishing of e-books, is a huge business. Writers and entrepreneurs of all types take advantage of the opportunity for digital self-publishing, both through blogs and e-books. Many people have parlayed success with these methods into bigger careers; some of them have even made fortunes.

The next section will discuss some of those people and how they used digital publishing tools to enhance their success. It will also discuss some ways that you might use and benefit from digital publishing in your life right now. Finally, it will look ahead to your future as a professional and discuss how digital publishing tools can help you begin to prepare for that future immediately.

CHAPTER TWO

DIGITAL PUBLISHING TODAY

The forms of digital publishing present in today's media landscape are bountiful, and new forms spring up all the time. People take for granted the constant online access to news, weather, and the latest gossip about celebrities and politicians. After the 2013 Academy Awards, the Internet was buzzing with gossip about Michelle Obama's appearance on the awards show. The First Lady addressed the digital gossip phenomenon in a statement to the Associated Press:

"Shoot, my bangs set off a national conversation," she said. "My shoes can set off a national conversation. That's just sort of where we are. We've got a lot of talking going on…It's like everybody's kitchen-table conversation

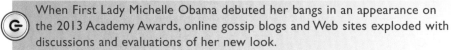

When First Lady Michelle Obama debuted her bangs in an appearance on the 2013 Academy Awards, online gossip blogs and Web sites exploded with discussions and evaluations of her new look.

is now accessible to everybody else, so there's a national conversation about anything." This public hunger for digital information, gossip, and conversation has created a huge demand for media outlets that provide those things. Forms of digital publishing satisfying this demand include online newspapers and magazines, blogs, and other independent journalism outlets. Here is a look at a few people who have been wildly successful in the digital publishing field and some of the tools available to make digital publishing accessible and convenient.

Blogging: Perez Hilton

Mario Armando Lavandeira Jr., a proud gay Cuban-American, was born March 23, 1978, in Miami. He

Mario Lavandeira Jr., better known as Perez Hilton, began blogging about celebrities as a hobby. His blog became extremely popular, making him a millionaire and a celebrity himself.

graduated with honors from New York University's Tisch School of the Arts in 2000, receiving a B.F.A. in drama. In 2004, he launched his blog, *PerezHilton.com* (originally called PageSixSixSix.com). In an interview with *Cliché* magazine in 2010, he revealed that although he was working in journalism when he launched his blog, he started the blog itself strictly as a hobby, rather than a business venture. "I started blogging purely as a hobby just for fun," said Hilton. "I discovered blogs and I wanted to try my hand at it. What set my site apart was that prior to PerezHilton.com, most blogs were mainly online journals and diaries, but that never interested me. I wanted to talk about celebrities because they're far more entertaining."

Hilton's pursuit of his hobby wound up revolutionizing the blogosphere and making him a multimillionaire and an international celebrity himself. *Forbes* magazine named him the #1 Web Celeb in 2007, 2008, and 2009, and *Hispanic* magazine named him 2009's Hispanic of the Year. His Web site currently receives three hundred million hits a month. Perez Hilton is a prime example of someone who turned a hobby in digital publishing into a wildly successful career.

Journalism: Nate Silver

Nate Silver is considered a political journalist. However, his career originated not from an interest in writing or politics, but from his love for baseball, statistics, and numbers, and a brief foray into the world of online gambling. Silver grew up in Michigan. In 1984, when he was six, the Detroit Tigers won the World Series. Silver

Nate Silver translated his love of statistics into a career as a political journalist. He became instantly famous when he correctly predicted the state-by-state results of the 2012 presidential election.

became a huge Tigers fan and began to apply his talent for math to baseball statistics. After graduating from the University of Chicago with a Bachelor of Arts in economics, he discovered online poker. Silver told the *Guardian* newspaper that poker taught him a lot about the role of chance in life. "And it gave me better training," he said, "than anything else I can think of about how to weigh new information, what might be important information and what might be less so."

Silver made an estimated $400,000 through online poker, money that he used to set up a Web site where he used existing data to make predictions about the careers of Major League Baseball players. Eventually, he began to look for other areas where he could apply his skill for predicting outcomes based on past and current numbers. That is when he discovered, and began to blog about, politics. In 2007, he set up a political blog that he named *FiveThirtyEight.com*, a reference to the 538 votes of the electoral college. During the 2012 presidential election, Silver predicted that Obama had a 90.9 percent chance of winning, while many other political pundits were saying it was too close to call. Silver was not only right about the overall outcome of the election, he also correctly predicted the winner in all fifty states. This impressed the media so much that Silver, a shy, openly gay, self-proclaimed geek, became a superstar basically overnight. His love of data, and the fact that he shared his systems and predictions through digital publishing, made him into another success story in the field.

Visit Nate Silver's blog, which covers sports statistics and political statistics. Silver originally published this blog independently, but it has been picked up by the *New York Times* and currently appears in the blog section of its Web site.

Self-Publishing: Amanda Hocking

Growing up in the countryside of Minnesota, teen paranormal-romance author Amanda Hocking did not have the happiest of childhoods. Her family was poor, her parents divorced when she was young, and she struggled with depression. Hocking found refuge and comfort in her voracious appetite for stories. She devoured books,

After receiving rejections from several traditional publishers over the years, Amanda Hocking became a self-made millionaire by digitally publishing her own teen paranormal-romance novels.

checking them out of the library and buying them at rummage sales. She had been telling her own stories since before she could even walk, and she soon began to write them down. By the age of twelve, Hocking was describing herself as a writer, and she completed her first novel at the age of seventeen. She sent the novel to several publishers, but received only rejection letters in return. This continued over the next several years, as Hocking wrote book after book, and they were all rejected by traditional publishers.

In April 2010, Hocking was working as a caretaker for disabled people, making only $18,000 a year. She desperately wanted to travel to Chicago to see an exhibition about Muppets creator Jim Henson, of whom she is a huge fan. She decided to self-publish a few of her books through Amazon Kindle, thinking that she could probably sell enough copies to family and friends to raise the $300 she needed for the trip to Chicago. She not only raised the money for the trip, but she also became a millionaire and a poster girl for self-publishing. Hocking has made over $2.5 million selling over 1.5 million books, and the traditional publishers who had rejected her novels for years quickly began to offer her deals to sign with them.

Current Digital Publishing Tools

There are constant advances in digital publishing, with new programs being developed and released all the time. Here are a few of the digital publishing tools currently available, with a brief description of the purposes they serve.

Adobe Digital Publishing Suite provides a convenient tool for many different types of large and small-scale publishing efforts. It can be used to digitally publish things like magazines, retail catalogs, and college brochures. It can also be used for one-time projects like pamphlets and portfolios. This tool can make digital publications interactive and educational, and it can be used without any special knowledge of digital code.

There are also many tools available for blogging. The oldest ones, such as LiveJournal, Blogger, and WordPress, are very convenient for text-based blogging, like keeping an online diary, and they are updated often with new features that make it easier to post visual content and link to other Web sites. According to

A Brief History of Blogging

The first blog *ever* was created by Justin Hall, a student at Swarthmore College, in 1994. The term "Web blog" was coined by John Barger in 1997. In 1999, Peter Merholz shortened the term to "blog," which is a portmanteau (a new word formed by combining two existing words). Barger's blog, like many early blogs, consisted of a list of links that kept record of the Internet sites he visited. Other early bloggers kept online diaries about their personal lives, or wrote about art, music, and literature. Before the development of blogging tools, online diaries were a part of personal Web sites. If you did not know much about HTML (the code used to write Web sites), it was difficult and time-consuming to make your entries appear in reverse chronological order. With the invention of early tools like Blogger and LiveJournal (both launched in 1999), blogging became much more convenient and accessible to people who were not very tech-savvy. Since then, blogging has become instrumental both in journalism, with blogs like the *Huffington Post*, and in social networking and entertainment, with celebrity-gossip blogs like Gawker. It has changed from a hobby into a profession. Many bloggers have had their blog concepts turned into books or have been hired to write for the blog sections of official news Web sites. Through the old standbys like Blogger and LiveJournal, and more recently launched sites like WordPress and Tumblr, the personal blog is still alive and well, too.

Andrew Lipsman on comScore, Tumblr is the most popular blogging tool among teens and college-aged users, with 50 percent of its users being under the age of twenty-five.

Rather than submitting manuscripts to agents and publishers, or paying the cost of printing and self-publishing physical books, many authors now choose to self-publish and sell their own work exclusively online, and some of them make a lot of money doing so. Amazon offers a tool called Kindle Direct Publishing, where authors can independently make their books available to Kindle users.

A CLOSER LOOK
Justin Hall's blog is officially considered the first personal blog ever and can still be found on the Internet. Although it includes modern elements like videos, it still has a very simple layout, reminiscent of the earliest personal Web sites.

CHAPTER THREE

DIGITAL PUBLISHING AND YOU

Whether they intend to or not, many teenagers use elements of digital publishing in their everyday expression and communication. This happens in informal, social sections of the Internet, as well as in academic situations. It occurs through personal blogs, Web sites, and online journals, and through school newspapers and literary magazines. Digital publishing touches many aspects of teen life, and there are lots of hobbies that can be useful, whether directly or indirectly, in launching a digital publishing career. This section will explore some of the ways that you may already use

Teenagers use digital publishing tools in many ways both at home and at school. For example, digital publishing tools are used often in journalism classes and in the production of school newspapers.

digital publishing and discuss hobbies that may provide avenues to a profession in the field. Considering these connections will help you make informed decisions regarding plans for your future after high school.

Using Digital Publishing Socially and Academically

Many teenagers create personal blogs or Web sites to share their thoughts with others, talk about things like movies and music, and sometimes share their writing or artwork. There are lots of tools, some of which have already been mentioned here, that make this type of publishing convenient. They all have different layouts and functions, and their usefulness varies depending on the user's purpose for blogging. For instance, Tumblr and Instagram are very popular with users who upload a lot of photographs, while sites like Blogger and LiveJournal remain popular with users who blog about their thoughts or experiences primarily in writing. People who combine both visual art and text often choose to develop their own Web sites. That kind of mixed format is more complicated and time-consuming than simply uploading a series of photos or typing into a box, but the versatility of expression that it allows makes it worthwhile for many teenagers.

WATCH OUT When posting to a blog, be careful how much personal information you share. If your blog is open to the public, do not share specific details such as your full name, your age, where you live, or where you go to school. If you do share personal details, make sure that your blog is visible only to people you know.

In addition to doing their own digital publishing, teenagers often encounter digital publishing at school.

These days, most school newspapers are produced, at least in part, through digital means. This also goes for literary magazines. Many newspapers and literary magazines are published online, and even if the final product is distributed in print, chances are that the design work was done using some kind of digital publishing tool. In addition, teachers are incorporating technology into the classroom in increasingly creative ways. For instance, you might be asked to design a newsletter or create a blog as a project for an English or social studies class. As technology becomes more and more common in schools, digital publishing will continue to be a part of the academic world.

Hobbies That Could Lead to a Career in Digital Publishing

Digital publishing is a part of many teenagers' lives, whether personally, academically, or both. There are many hobbies and interests that can translate into a career in the field of digital publishing. The hobbies detailed below are definitely not the only ones that can relate to the field, but they are the ones that offer the most direct applications.

Creative writing is one of the hobbies most obviously connected to digital publishing. If you write novels or short fiction as a hobby, you might find success self-publishing them digitally, like Amanda Hocking. If you are a poet or if you enjoy writing about your personal life, you could start your own blog, which, if it becomes popular and widely recognized, could lead to a book deal. Or once you compile enough material for a book, you could go the self-publishing route.

An interest in current events is another hobby that could easily translate into a digital publishing career. Whether you enjoy following political news, sports, or the latest celebrity gossip, there are many ways you can use digital means to turn your hobby into future success. You could use one of the many free blogging tools to begin keeping track of and publishing your knowledge and insights. This way, you could start building a Web presence with the eventual goal of being hired by a professional online magazine or newspaper.

Amateur photographers can also use digital publishing tools to turn their hobby into a profession. Blogging tools like Tumblr allow amateur photographers

Digital cameras, cell phone cameras, and photo-sharing services such as Instagram have made photography a popular hobby for teenagers. Some people are able to translate their hobbies into careers as professional photographers.

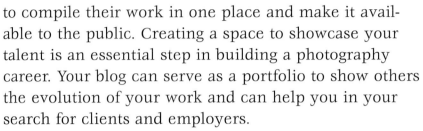
to compile their work in one place and make it available to the public. Creating a space to showcase your talent is an essential step in building a photography career. Your blog can serve as a portfolio to show others the evolution of your work and can help you in your search for clients and employers.

A talent for graphic arts can lead to a career in digital publishing as well. Even with all of the tools available for designing digital magazines, newspapers, and brochures, it still takes creativity to make decisions about which format to use and how the publication should look. Many companies want to hire someone who has a keen eye for things like design, color, and layout.

Another hobby that figures into the digital publishing field is computer programming. You might not initially associate this more scientific hobby with the creative hobbies mentioned here, but it is essential for digital publishing. All of the tools and programs that make digital publishing convenient have to be written by computer programmers, so a love of computers and programming could turn into a career writing the programs that make digital publishing possible.

TECH TOOLS Adobe's Web site not only offers tutorials and user forums to help with technical issues, but it also includes a blog that gives updates on innovative uses of their products and a gallery of publications created using Digital Publishing Suite. This is a great resource, both for tech support and for inspiration.

Copyright Laws: Protecting Yourself and Your Work

Having the copyright to your work means that you have authority over the ways your work can be reproduced and distributed. Both published and unpublished works can be copyrighted, including works of literature (which include computer programs) and pieces of art or music. It is not necessary to register with the government in order to obtain copyright over your original work; as soon as it is created, you already own the rights to it. Registration (which can be done easily online or through the mail at any point after the work is created) has some benefits, especially if you ever have to go to court to defend your copyright. However, it is important to know that your work is protected under the law even if it is not registered. Other people need your permission to reproduce your work either in print or digitally, to distribute it for sale, to prepare new works that are based on your work, and to display or perform it publicly. If they do any of these things without your permission, it is a violation of copyright. You do not have to be an adult to claim copyright; minors own the rights to their own original work. Your work is legally protected whether or not you include a copyright notice, but it is wise to include one. This will prevent people from being able to claim that they did not realize the work was copyrighted. Copyright notice can be very easily indicated using the copyright symbol (the letter c in a circle), the year the work was created or published, and the owner's name.

Translating Your Hobby into Future Success

When you are looking to turn a hobby into a career, one of the most important things to consider is professional experience. Often this experience is gained through internships or part-time jobs during high school and college. Whether you are a writer, a photographer, a budding journalist, a graphic designer, or a computer programmer, there are jobs and internships relevant to your field. A part-time job at a printer or a copy shop could serve as a step into graphic design, for instance, and a summer internship working for a magazine could be wonderful experience for a writer, journalist, or photographer. It is important to begin thinking of your work

When considering a career, it is helpful to meet people who are professionals in that field. Part-time jobs, internships, and networking are three ways to make those connections.

as a profession, rather than simply a hobby. So the sooner you can begin work in the field, the better.

Choosing a college major is another important step toward becoming a professional. It is wise to have an idea of what you want to study before you even begin looking at colleges because this can help you narrow your search to schools that have strong programs in the field you want to enter. If you are interested in digital publishing, you might choose a school that is strong in art (for photography or graphic design), one that has a reputable English program (for literature or journalism), or a school that specializes in technology (for computer programming). Choosing your major wisely will help make your career path more direct.

There are several reasons why it is helpful to have a specific career in mind when making decisions about your future schooling—or your future in general. Although it is important not to limit yourself when you are young, it is also unwise to waste time and money on a college major that you will ultimately switch or a degree that you will not use. Having a career, or at least a specific field, in mind can help prevent this. When you choose a field that will allow you to use the hobbies and interests you already have, there is a much better chance that you will stay motivated to continue along the path to your selected career.

CHAPTER FOUR
FOCUSING AND REFINING YOUR GOALS

Having a specific career (or even a general professional field) in mind is a wonderful first step toward future success and security. The next step is to focus your interest and enthusiasm, and begin to take concrete measures to achieve your goals. There are certain developments that are necessary and beneficial no matter what field a person hopes to enter. This section will look at some of those developments, such as beginning to see yourself as a professional, building a résumé and portfolio, and choosing a college major, and will give you advice on how to begin doing those things now. Keep in mind that digital publishing tools can be helpful for things like building

Creating a résumé is an important step in the process of searching for a job and building a career. Résumés should be straightforward and easy to understand, not cluttered with unnecessary information.

portfolios and résumés, no matter what career you are pursuing.

Becoming a Professional

The word "professional" has a few different meanings. We tend to think of a professional as someone who has a lot of training and who is already making money in his or her field, and that is certainly one of the meanings of the word. But *Merriam-Webster* also describes the adjective "professional" as meaning "characterized by or conforming to the technical or ethical standards of a profession" and "exhibiting a courteous, conscientious, and generally businesslike manner in the workplace." You can pursue these aspects of being a professional whether or not you are making money in your field and regardless of your level of training or experience. The more you begin to behave as a professional, the more likely others will be to view you as one, and this will be instrumental in building your career. You should strive for professionalism in all of your interactions, whether you are working at a part-time job or internship, seeking information from a college recruiter, or simply having a conversation with someone in your field. Professionalism includes knowing the jargon (specific language and technical terms) used in your field, so it is a good idea to research those things. When you hear a term you are unfamiliar with, look it up or ask someone what it means.

Building a Résumé

One thing that every professional needs is a résumé. Creating one can be a daunting task, especially if you begin when you already have several jobs and other pursuits in your history. You can stay a step ahead by beginning a résumé as soon as possible, then adding to it and amending it as your experience changes. It is important, however, to remember that your résumé is a small part of the job search process and that its primary purpose is simply to get you noticed.

As Tony Beshara, author of *Unbeatable Résumés*, said in an interview with *Forbes* magazine, "Here's the truth—it is rare to get hired by simply submitting a résumé—the purpose of a résumé is to help you get an interview." Agonizing too much over a résumé is a waste of time, and including too much information can actually harm your chances of being interviewed. Beshara went on to give several tips about résumé writing, saying that résumés should be simple, straightforward, and easily understood by someone inside or outside the field. He recommended avoiding fancy fonts and formats, and opting for Times New Roman and a very simple layout. He also said that it is best to omit summaries, objectives, and unnecessary personal information. These things all distract potential employers from the information in which they are primarily interested: where you have worked and what you did there.

QUICK TIP

Most word processing programs come equipped with templates for résumés. Rather than trying to format your own résumé, you can save time by finding a simple design and plugging in your information.

For any young person seeking a career in the digital publishing field, it is important to create a portfolio of past and current work that can be taken to interviews.

Creating a Portfolio

When seeking a career in a field that involves writing or art, it is useful to have a portfolio of the work you have done previously. You can take your portfolio with you to interviews, and it can serve as a concise way to show potential employers or college recruiters your style and accomplishments. If you have previously shared your work on a blog, then you are already a step ahead in creating a portfolio. You can look through the work on your blog and the comments you have received, and select the things that you feel best represent your talent. You can also list the blog among your accomplishments. However, even if you have not previously published your work online, you can still compile it in order to present it during a job or college search. Tools like Adobe Digital Publishing Suite can be useful in creating an attractive and professional-looking portfolio. The more time and effort you put into your portfolio, the more likely it is to reflect professionalism and competence. Your portfolio should be an ongoing project, and as you develop, you should add new elements and remove things that are no longer relevant.

Networking

Networking is defined as "the cultivation of productive relationships for employment or business." This is one of the most important aspects of professional life, although for many people, it is also the most difficult. Some people are shy and find it hard to approach others both socially and professionally. Other people may worry about seeming opportunistic, as though they are taking advantage of others for personal gain, or sounding as though they are bragging about their own accomplishments. However, even if you have misgivings about networking, it is an essential skill and practice for any professional. You will have to figure out methods of networking that feel natural and come easily to you, and sometimes you will have to push yourself out of your comfort zone.

The more you practice networking, the easier it will become. A good way to start is by taking a genuine interest in the accomplishments of other people in your field. When you ask questions and offer compliments regarding their achievements, it may become easier to talk about your own interests and pursuits. This will lay a good foundation for asking questions and seeking advice about your own work. Remember, everyone in your field had to start somewhere, and they all had to network, too.

WATCH OUT It is important to network safely and wisely. Never give out your phone number or address to a stranger, and never meet someone from the Internet in person unless it is in a public place and you are accompanied by a parent or guardian. Try to network with your peers and with mentors that you meet through school and related activities.

What If I Don't Want to Go to College?

There is no question that higher education is very useful both professionally and personally, but the reality is that not everyone wants to go to college—and not everyone has to. Although a college degree will help you, it would be false to say that you cannot find success without one. Digital publishing is a field in which it may be possible to find success without a college degree. Self-publishing, for instance, requires no particular credentials. You can write and publish novels without any formal training, and if they find a large audience, you can make a lot of money. However, the decision not to go to college should be an informed and intentional one, just like the decision to go to college should be. It is not something that should be settled on or decided lightly, simply because you do not want to go through the hassle of filling out applications.

Before making a decision about college, you should have a clear idea of a profession you want to pursue. You should weigh the pros and cons of having a college degree in that profession, and explore the likelihood of finding success without one. There may be other forms of training, such as trade school or alternative certification programs, that can serve the same purpose as a degree program could serve. If that is the case, then college may not be a necessity. Or you may decide that you want to work or travel for a few years and go to college after that. Not everyone has to follow the same schedule or path to achieving success. However, regardless of your choice, you need to have a clear and intentional path in mind for the future. All of your decisions should be made with careful planning and consideration of their possible outcomes.

Part-Time Jobs, Internships, and College

As mentioned in the previous section, one way you can begin to pursue your career goals is to look for part-time jobs or internships in a related field. High school can be an ideal time to do this. While most people are in high school, their parents or guardians provide them with basics like shelter, food, and clothing, so they have the freedom to seek employment as a way to get ahead, rather than a way to pay for necessities. Once you have finished college and are living on your own, most likely making payments on your student loans, it will be much harder to take a job that pays little or nothing simply to get experience in your field. If you are able to think ahead and try to do this now, you will have an advantage when you reach that point in your life. If it is a financial necessity that you work during high school, you can definitely still try to connect your employment to your future goals. Even if you have to take a job that initially is unrelated, you can continue to search for one that will meet your needs and offer experience in your future field.

A college degree is an advantage in a lot of fields and a necessity in some. If you plan to earn a degree, it is never too early to begin preparing and planning for college. There are many ways to do this. You can begin by putting your best efforts toward your academic and extracurricular pursuits in high school. Excellent grades and participation in school activities outside the class-room look good on all college applications. It will be

Finding a part-time job or an internship in the field you hope to enter is a valuable way to gain training and experience. High school is a great time to do this.

especially helpful if you choose activities that relate to the field you hope to enter. For instance, if you want to go to school for journalism, you should get involved with your high school newspaper. Begin researching colleges as soon as possible, so you can find out which ones offer programs that sound exciting to you. Then you can find out their admission requirements and make sure you are on the right track to be accepted. You will save a lot of time and energy by narrowing your college search to schools that suit your interests and future plans.

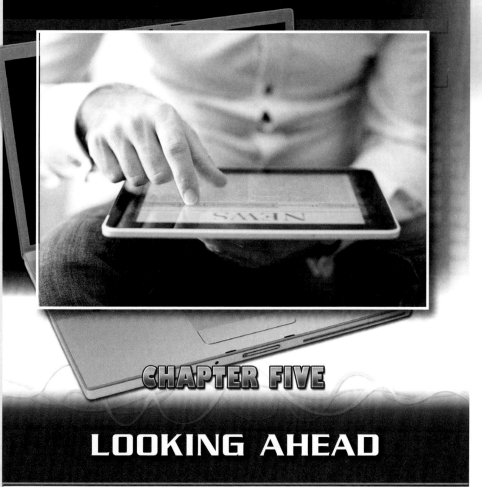

CHAPTER FIVE

LOOKING AHEAD

With all this emphasis on setting clear and specific career goals, it is necessary to give an overview of several careers using digital publishing tools. When considering any career, or making any decision at all, it helps to examine both the advantages and the disadvantages. For all of the careers examined in this section, there will be a brief description of the career itself and a discussion of the pros and the cons. Following the list of careers, there will be some tips on how you can apply the career-building advice from the previous section specifically to this field and a few more suggestions for building toward a future career in digital publishing. All of these things will help you define your goals so that

Professional writing and journalism are two possible careers in digital publishing for those who enjoy and are skilled at writing. Both of these careers often allow you to work independently.

you can begin to work toward them. Planning and taking deliberate actions toward your goals is a key factor in establishing yourself as a professional.

Writing

If you already enjoy writing as a hobby, you should definitely consider it as a career. The digital revolution has made literature of all kinds more widely available, and with so many new devices and formats for reading, there is a high demand for reading material.

There are plenty of pros to a career as a writer. If you write fiction, poetry, or creative essays, you get to express your artistic talent. If you write informational text, you get to develop the technical aspects of your writing and learn how to communicate your thoughts clearly and persuasively. As a professional writer, you get to work at your own pace, and you usually get to choose where you work. Writers often work from home, in cafés, or even outside.

 Many professional writers use Web sites to find freelance work. Elance.com is an example of a Web site that connects writers with people who are looking to hire them on a contracted basis, meaning that they will be paid a fixed amount for an agreed-upon project.

Journalism

Another possible career in digital publishing is journalism. Journalism can often provide a steadier income than other forms of writing, especially if you are able to find employment with a large publication, like an established magazine or newspaper. Because of technological advancements, the world of journalism is constantly changing. This can serve as both a pro and a con when considering a career in the field.

Technology has made it easier for people to engage in amateur journalism through personal blogs or through the comments sections of news outlets. Because it is easy to participate in the field as an amateur, it may also be easier to get your foot in the door as a professional. Many people who are interested in journalism, especially in the digital field, start out as bloggers. Sometimes they publish their blogs independently, and other times they are hired to blog for a specific news outlet. If the blog is successful enough, its writer may be hired as a regular columnist.

The changing nature of journalism could also be a con, however. Because so much news is shared in real time through personal blogs and outlets like Twitter, the number of jobs for traditional news reporters may decrease. This does not have to be a deterrent to a career in the field, but it does mean that you will need to be creative and proactive in order to find steady work.

Photography

Photography can be a great career through which to participate in the digital publishing field, with similar pros and cons to a writing career. A photographer has a lot of flexibility with the way he or she works, and digital publishing makes this flexibility even greater. If you work

Professional photographers are in high demand for important events such as weddings. Digital publishing helps these professionals promote their businesses and also helps clients share their photos with friends and family.

as a professional photographer for events like weddings, graduations, and family portraits, digital publishing tools can help you promote your business and offer clients creative ways to share their photos. Another possibility is to work as a photojournalist, who covers news or entertainment events by taking pictures. Many online news outlets hire photographers as well as writers. Photography can offer the freedom of working for yourself or the security of working for a company, either of which can be a huge pro.

Graphic Design

Graphic design is an essential part of digital publishing. The aspects of graphic design involved in digital publications include visual art, typography (the way the words look and are arranged on the page), page layout, and Web and software design. Because graphic design includes both artistic and technical elements, it offers opportunities to people who are inclined in either of those areas and is especially well-suited to people who have talent in both. Graphic design has room for artists and computer programmers alike.

Building Toward Your Career Now

There are many ways that you can immediately begin building toward your career in digital publishing. All of the career tips discussed in earlier sections can be directly applied to the careers mentioned in this section.

Whether you aspire to be a writer, journalist, photographer, or graphic designer, you can begin to preserve your work through a Web site or in a portfolio. Digital publishing tools are very helpful for doing this. One option is to create a blog through Tumblr, WordPress, or another blogging tool, and add your work to the blog as you create it. If you are a visual arts person, your blog posts will mostly be the photos you have taken or pictures of your designs. Journalists and other writers can share their latest projects through blogs as well. Another idea is to create a portfolio using digital publishing tools to present your work in the format of a brochure or magazine.

It is important to draw attention to your work if you want to become a successful professional. Blogging through services such as Tumblr can be a great way to share your work and to begin building a following.

All the blogging tools mentioned here provide support for designing your page and creating the layout that best suits the information or artwork you want to present. They also provide instructions for things such as uploading files and changing the order in which your posts appear.

Your Internet Footprint

When trying to build a career in digital publishing or any other field, it is important to keep your "Internet footprint" in mind. Just like you leave a record of footprints when you walk through mud, sand, or snow, you leave a record of your activities on the Internet. Potential employers and even college admissions officers may look at this record when they are deciding whether or not to accept you for employment or admission. For this reason, it is essential to be careful about the things that appear on the Internet attached to your name. You want to be sure that when someone looks you up, they get a good impression from the things they see. To get an idea of what your Internet footprint currently looks like, try typing your name into a search engine. Take a close look at the first items that appear. Are they things that you would want an employer to see? Do they portray you in a professional manner? If you are not sure, have an adult that you trust take a look as well and give you his or her opinion. You want to give the impression that you take yourself seriously and that your work is important to you. If an employer sees only pictures or videos of you goofing off with friends and no evidence that you aspire to work in the field, he or she may not get that impression. It can be very hard to think ahead like this when you are in high school, but if you take the time to be careful with your Internet presence, you will be very happy you did. As technology advances, more and more of your Internet activities will be traceable, and employers and recruiters will definitely take advantage of that technology.

You can immediately begin developing the professional habits you will need to master in your career. These habits include meeting deadlines, editing your work, and striving for excellence. Even before anyone begins to pay you for your work as a writer, photographer, or designer, you can set deadlines for yourself so that you get used to working under pressure. One idea is to look for contests to enter. This will not only help you work toward a specific date, but it will also motivate you to edit your own work and make the changes that take it from good to excellent. These are all essential habits for a career in digital publishing.

Another thing you should begin doing as soon as possible is networking. Look for people whose work you admire and reach out to those people. Share your own work with them, and ask them for advice in getting your career started. Find out the steps those people took to get to where they are professionally, and cultivate relationships with them. You never know what opportunities will arise from those relationships.

Finally, get as many people interested in your work as possible. The Internet is the best way to do this. Once you have created a blog or a Web site to showcase your work, share it with everyone you know, and ask people to share it with their friends as well. Social networking is a very useful way to reach a wide audience. This can help with all of the other aspects of your career, especially networking. The more people have the chance to see and admire your work, the more likely they will take an interest in helping you along your professional path.

GLOSSARY

amateur Someone who engages in the study or practice of something as a hobby rather than as a profession.

blog An online diary or a record of personal observations about a particular subject, organized in individually dated entries.

blogosphere The online community of bloggers and the ways in which they connect with each other.

copyright The legal right governing the reproduction and distribution of a work of art, music, or literature.

e-book A book in digital form containing text, images, or both, designed to be viewed on a computer screen or an e-reader.

e-reader A handheld electronic device that displays books, magazines, and newspapers in digital form. Examples include the Amazon Kindle and the Barnes & Noble Nook.

freelancer A person who works independently for different employers, usually for specific projects or fixed amounts of time.

HTML Hypertext markup language, the main language used to create Web pages.

interface The way a computer program communicates with users and with other programs and devices.

Internet footprint The record of your online activities as it appears to the public.

internship On-the-job training, usually unpaid.

jargon The language and technical terms specific to a professional field.

layout The arrangement and style of the content on a page.

literary magazine A periodical publication, often put out by high schools and colleges, containing short stories, poetry, and essays.

networking Cultivating relationships for the purpose of moving ahead in your profession.

portfolio A collection of recent work designed to demonstrate your competence in a particular field.

public domain When the copyright on a work has expired and it can be reproduced and distributed freely.

résumé A summary of one's work history and experience.

self-publishing Making one's work available publicly, often for sale, without the assistance of an agent or a publishing company.

trade school A school that offer instruction in a specific trade or technical skill.

typography The style and arrangement of printed words on a page.

FOR MORE INFORMATION

Association of American Publishers (AAP)
455 Massachusetts Avenue NW, Suite 700
Washington, DC 20001-2777
(202) 347-3375
Web site: http://www.publishers.org
With more than two hundred thousand members, the
AAP brings together publishers of all types, including academic, commercial, and professional, and
includes nonprofits, independents, and university
presses. It advocates for publishers and represents
the industry on issues such as copyright, technology, tax, literacy, and censorship.

Association of Canadian Publishers (ACP)
174 Spadina Avenue, Suite 306
Toronto, ON M5T 2C2
Canada
(416) 487-6116
Web site: http://www.publishers.ca
The ACP consists of Canadian-owned publishing companies spanning many different genres. It is
committed to sustaining the vitality of Canadian
publishing through research, marketing, professional development, and public relations.

Canadian Career Development Foundation (CCDF)
119 Ross Avenue, Suite 202
Ottawa, ON K1Y 0N6

Canada

Web site: http://www.ccdf.ca

The CCDF is a nonprofit that advocates for worker satis-
faction and productivity and for services that
prepare youth for the workforce and ongoing learn-
ing. The association's Web site provides training
materials and resources for career development
professionals working with youth and adults.

International Publishers Association (IPA)

23, avenue de France

1202 Geneva, Switzerland

+41 22 704 18 20

Web site: http://www.internationalpublishers.org

Founded in 1896 in Paris, the IPA is comprised of publishers' associations representing Africa, Asia,
Europe, and the Americas. The association is committed to defending the freedom of expression and
to defending copyright law, and serves as a meeting
place where publishers can network and converse
about the issues affecting their field.

National Career Development Association (NCDA)

305 N. Beech Circle

Broken Arrow, OK 74012

(91) 663-7060

Web site: http://www.ncda.org

A division of the American Counseling Association, the
NCDA serves career development professionals and
the general public. The association's Web site con-
tains resources, information, and tools regarding
career development issues such as job searching,

education, salary information, and employment trends. The resources section of its Web site has a section specifically for youth and young adults.

Online Publishers Association (OPA)
1350 Broadway, Suite 606
New York, NY 10018
(646) 473-1000
Web site: http://www.online-publishers.org
A nonprofit organization, the OPA was founded in June 2001. It has a U.S. branch and a European branch. The organization conducts research into the latest development and trends in online marketing in order to help its members compete in the digital publishing industry.

Web Sites

Due to the changing nature of Internet links, Rosen Publishing has developed an online list of Web sites related to the subject of this book. This site is updated regularly. Please use this link to access the list:

http://www.rosenlinks.com/DCB/DPT

FOR FURTHER READING

Alvear, Michael. *Make a Killing on Kindle (Without Blogging, Facebook or Twitter): The Guerilla Marketer's Guide to Selling Ebooks on Amazon.* Kindle Edition, 2012.

Beatty, Kelly, and Dale Bradshaw. *Firestarters: 100 Job Profiles to Inspire Young Women.* Seattle, WA: CreateSpace, 2012.

Bolles, Richard, and Carol Christen. *What Color Is Your Parachute? For Teens, 2nd Ed.: Discovering Yourself, Defining Your Future.* New York, NY: Ten Speed Press, 2012.

Cramsie, Patrick. *The Story of Graphic Design: From the Invention of Writing to the Birth of Digital Design.* New York, NY: Abrams Books, 2010.

Dangerlove, Daphne. *The Self-Publishing Toolkit: How to Publish and Sell Kindle eBooks on Amazon.* Dangerlove Productions: Kindle Edition, 2012.

Dorch, Patricia. *Job Search: Teen Interview Tips and Strategies to Get Hired.* Murietta, CA: ExecuDress, 2012.

Heller, Stephen, and Lita Talarico, eds. *Typography Sketchbook.* New York, NY: Princeton Architectural Press, 2011.

Kalmbach, Mike. *Writing Advice for Teens: Creating Stories.* Seattle, WA: CreateSpace, 2012.

MacGregor, Cynthia. *When I Grow Up, I Want to Be a Writer.* Portland, OR: ReadHowYouWant, 2012.

McKesson, Nellie. *Publishing with iBooks Author.* Boston, MA: Tools of Change, 2012.

McLeod, Marilyn. *Secrets of Self-Publishing*. Seattle, WA: CreateSpace, 2010.

Minger, Elda. *The Virgin's Guide to Writing Your First Romance Novel*. Kindle Edition, 2012.

Peterson's Publishing. *Teens' Guide to College and Career Planning*. Paramus, NJ: Peterson's, 2011.

Pipps, Karen G. *The Absolute Blogging How-To Handbook for New Bloggers*. Seattle, WA: CreateSpace, 2011.

Potter, Ellen. *Spilling Ink: A Young Writer's Handbook*. New York, NY: Square Fish, 2010.

Schuman, Nancy. *1,001 Phrases You Need to Get a Job: The Hire Me Words That Set Your Cover Letter, Resume and Job Interview Apart*. New York, NY: Adams Media, 2012.

Seddon, Tony. *Graphic Design for Nondesigners*. San Francisco, CA: Chronicle Books, 2009.

Thomas, Isabel. *Being a Photographer* (On the Radar: Awesome Jobs). Minneapolis, MN: Lerner Publications, 2012.

Yardley, Kathy. *Rock Your Plot: A Simple System for Plotting Your Novel*. Kindle Edition, 2012.

Zielen, Lara. *Make Things Happen: The Key to Networking for Teens*. Portland, OR: ReadHowYouWant, 2012.

BIBLIOGRAPHY

Cadwalladr, Carole. "Nate Silver: It's the Numbers, Stupid." *Guardian*, November 17, 2012. Retrieved March 18, 2013 (http://www.guardian.co .uk/world/2012/nov/17/nate-silver-interview -election-data-statistics).

CelebrityNetWorth.com. "Perez Hilton Net Worth." Retrieved March 10, 2013 (http://www .celebritynetworth.com/richest-celebrities/perez -hilton-net-worth).

Cliché Magazine. "Perez Hilton: A Digital Media Phenomenon." June/July 2010. Retrieved March 10, 2013 (http://www.clichemag.com/wp -content/uploads/past_issues/June _July2010issue.pdf).

Cowles, Charlotte. "Michelle Obama Brushes Off Criticism About Oscars, Bangs." *New York Magazine*, March 1, 2013. Retrieved March 18, 2013 (http://www.celeblatest.com/fashion-news/ michelle-obama-brushes-criticism-over-oscars -bangs#.Ucuo65yBMvo).

Hannon, Kerry. "Want An Unbeatable Resume? Read These Tips from a Top Recruiter." *Forbes Magazine*, August 24, 2011. Retrieved March 10, 2013 (http:// www.forbes.com/sites/kerryhannon/2011/08/24/ want-an-unbeatable-resume-read-these-tips-from-a -top-recruiter).

Lipsman, Andrew. "Tumblr Defines Its Name as User Growth Accelerates." August 30, 2011. Retrieved

March 27, 2013 (http://www.comscore.com/
Insights/Blog/Tumblr_Defies_its_Name_as_User
_Growth_Accelerates).

PerezHilton.com. "Bio-Who Is Perez Hilton?" Retrieved
March 10, 2013 (http://www.comscore.com/
Insights/Blog/Tumblr_Defies_its_Name_as_User
_Growth_Accelerates).

Pickington, Ed. "Amanda Hocking, the Writer Who Made
Millions by Self-Publishing Online." *Guardian*,
January 12, 2012. Retrieved March 10, 2013 (http://
www.guardian.co.uk/books/2012/jan/12/amanda
-hocking-self-publishing).

Thompson, Clive. "A Timeline of the History of
Blogging." *New York Magazine*, February 20, 2006.
Retrieved March 26, 2013 (http://nymag.com/
news/media/15971).

U.S. Copyright Office. "Copyright Basics." May 2012.
Retrieved March 26, 2013 (www.copyright.gov).

Wortham, Jenna. "After 10 Years of Blogs, the Future's
Brighter Than Ever." *Wired*, December 17, 2007.
Retrieved March 26, 2013.

INDEX

A

Adobe Digital Publishing Suite, 20, 28, 37
alternative certifications, 39

B

Barger, John, 21
Blogger, 20, 21, 25
blogging, 4, 5, 12, 20–21, 25–27, 37, 46, 48, 49
  history of, 21
  profiles of bloggers, 14–18

C

careers
  creating a résumé, 32, 34–35
  cultivating a professional attitude, 34, 37, 51
  importance of networking, 37–38, 51
  and portfolios, 28, 32, 34, 37, 48
  preparing for, 26–31
  what you can do now, 48–49, 51
  without college, 39
CD-ROM, 8, 9
college, 31, 32, 34, 37, 39, 40–42, 50

computer programming, 6, 28, 30, 31, 48
contests, 51
copyright laws, 7, 8, 29
creative writing, 26–27, 30, 31, 39, 45, 48, 51
current events (interest in as path to a career), 27

D

digital footprint, 50
digital publishing
  and copyright, 7, 8, 29
  current uses, 11–12
  history of, 6–9
  and privacy, 25, 38
  and social networking, 12, 25
  tools, 6, 12, 20–22, 32, 43
  use in school, 5, 11–12, 25–26

E

e-book, evolution of the, 7–8
Elance.com, 45

F

FiveThirtyEight.com, 18
freelance work, 45

About the Author

Rebecca Klein writes books for young adults. She enjoys singing, cooking, and playing outside. Klein is currently working on a master's degree in English education. She grew up in Detroit and lives in Brooklyn.

Photo Credits

Cover, pp. 1, 4, 13, 23, 32, 43 (laptop) © iStockphoto.com/Lisa Thornberg; cover, p. 1 (laptop screen, tablet) © iStockphoto .com/daboost; cover, p.1 (books, e-reader) © iStockphoto.com/ Bosca78; cover, interior pages (mouse) © iStockphoto.com/ abu; p. 4 (inset) © iStockphoto.com/pictafolio; p. 5 Till Jacket/ Photononstop/Getty Images; p. 7 ClassicStock.com/ SuperStock; p. 9 Science & Society Picture Library/Getty Images; p. 10 Francois Lochon/Gamma-Rapho/Getty Images; p. 13 (inset) © iStockphoto.com/RapidEye; 14 Chris Pizzello/ Invision/AP Images; p. 15 Earl Gibson III/Getty Images; p. 17 Amy E. Price/Getty Images; pp. 19, 24 © AP Images; p. 23 (inset) © iStockphoto.com/Alejandro Rivera; p. 27 Felix Mizioznikov/Shutterstock.com; p. 30 PhotoAlto/Laurence Mouton/Getty Images; p. 32 (inset) © iStockphoto.com/ badahos; p. 33 Image Source/Getty Images; p. 36 © iStockphoto.com/Izabela Habur; p. 41 Peter Dazeley/The Image Bank/Getty Images; p. 43 (inset) © iStockphoto.com/ StudioThreeDots; p. 44 ollyy/Shutterstock.com; p. 47 Sonnenschein/Report Digital-REA/Redux; p. 49 Jens Büttner/picture-alliance/dpa/AP Images; cover and interior pages background patterns and graphics © iStockphoto.com/ Ali Mazraie Shadi, © iStockphoto.com/MISHA, © iStockphoto .com/Paul Hill, © iStockphoto.com/Charles Taylor, © iStockphoto.com/Daniel Halvorson, © iStockphoto.com/ Jeffrey Sheldon.

Designer: Nelson Sa; Editor: Bethany Bryan;
Photo Researcher: Marty Levick